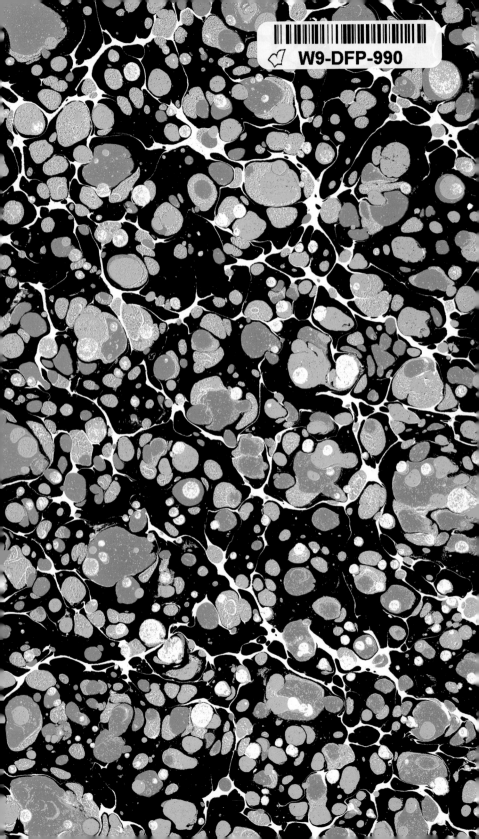

To Dad –

hope that you find
this poetry inspiring
for your own!

Love,

Rachel & Wayne
xo

Man in Love

Man in Love • Richard Outram

The Porcupine's Quill, Inc.

Published by the Porcupine's Quill, 68 Main Street, Erin,
Ontario N0B 1T0 with the financial assistance of the
Canada Council and the Ontario Arts Council.

Distributed in Canada and the United States by Firefly
Books, 3520 Pharmacy Avenue, Unit 1C, Scarborough,
Ontario M1W 2T8.

Some of these poems were previously published by
Canadian Literature, The Compass, Exile, The Gauntlet Press and
Toronto Life.

Typeset in Joanna by The Coach House Press (Toronto).
Printed on Zephyr Antique laid, sewn into signatures and
bound in March, 1985 by the Porcupine's Quill.

Cover and interior wood engravings by Barbara Howard.

ISBN 0-88984-069-5

This book is for

Barbara

She is abstracted, she may perish because
An ebony cat in the wild orchard, turning
Into a blaze of sunlight seems not to pause,
Passing from cobalt shadow to black burning.

Elephant Folio

First Philosopher:
    Oho! This page is a perfect blank; therefore
    it follows, as blank night blankest day,
    that the whole boiling, the vast shebang
    has yet to be written down.

Second Philosopher:
    Here is a palimpsest; which proceeds, like life,
    every which way. A snarl, a swarm, a confusion;
    and even its vestiges, remnants, erasures must
    be studied to be deciphered.

Third Philosopher:
    This is a hodgepodge, a shuffle, a scramble
    of manuscript leaves, a looseleaf, a volume
    still to be bound. The problem is sequence;
    the question one of collation.

Fourth Philosopher:
    We have before us the Hansard of Babel.
    As it might be, Linear X. We are set,
    for our sins, to the sometime heroic, probable
    impossible task of translation.

Fifth Philosopher:
   The total poem of this world, set forth
   in its primal, seamless, hypnotic flow,
   sans punctuation. We have to discover,
   distinguish from accidence, syntax.

Sixth Philosopher:
   The text, scholars, is present: it is obscure.
   Bring rubric, lemma, scholium, scruple: the mind,
   pertinacious, employs the apparatus of order.
   We must wax lyrical-exegetical.

Seventh Philosopher:
   Brothers: our father, remember, was also
   a seventh son: the universe of words, to be sure,
   possessed him. He had it entire by heart.
   Commence, with exuberance, dalliance.

Dr. Dolittle

Almost unable in the text
To bear with what was coming next,

How could I ever hope to know,
Once having been abandoned so,

The elegant, insistent why
And wherefore whereby I was I,

The creature of my tender years,
And not the other of my fears?

As yet, I only knew, I knew,
Although I knew it through and through,

That one must somehow, in the end,
Become and thereby comprehend,

Embody and elaborate
The tale that no one would relate

To me: whereof the central part
I had complete, I thought, by heart;

But guessed with surety I had
The best of reasons to be glad,

As long as I was child, not Man,
That one was not allowed to scan

The scientific occult note;
The answer the good Doctor wrote

With feverish delighted haste,
That not an inkling go to waste,

Upon the silken lining torn
Out of his hat, while he was borne,

As all of us, perhaps, may be,
Across the bottom of the sea

Within the great snail's chambered shell:
And understood therein full well

The question he had died to ask
The mollusc, being brought to task

Before the pushmi-pullyu's rare,
Binary relentless stare.

Genesis

Somewhere behind the morning, unbeknownst,
She gave sudden approval. And Love assumed
Form specific before him again, and again:
A thorn tree; a lichen ring; the undulant groomed

Weed in the stream returning upon itself;
An equation of farm roofs. And under duress
Once more and embarrassed in his remove
He bent to pick some spatulate watercress.

The water shocked him, cold, burning his wrist.
He was minded of childhood and earlier hidden springs.
A fingerling trout, flicked into shadow; and one shard's
Glint; and the equipoised isinglass wings

Of a darning needle frozen upon a stone
Like a turquoise vein; and his own blurred
Reflection that shrank away as he straightened up
Weighing a strange phrase, an estranged Word.

Round of Life

Let us the fruit of Love's pursuit
discover;
Of Jenny Wren, of speckled hen,
of plover.

Here is an egg. Without a leg
to stand on:
When laid to rest, it must the nest
abandon.

Death is the norm: this perfect form
before us
We contemplate, may to our fate
restore us.

Herein is held, without a weld,
or caulking,
A germ of flight, '... world of delight,'
& squawking:

Which is, when broached, & sometime poached,
devoured;
That thereby we may likewise be
empowered.

Riddles for Old Cameron

Sometimes both up and down, I rise
On high to stoop; sometimes disguise
Both friend and foe; sometimes, when worn,
Am both discarded and adorn.

Mortal, time may see us crazed;
Meanwhile, reflect on being blazed,
By my fidelity amazed.

Each one of us a trinity,
My maker walked at length with me
And getting nowhere, laid me by
For life or death. If I am I
When I am not, you comprehend:
In my beginning is my end.

For sober, superstitious souls,
My solace must seem full of holes.
A garner of collectives knows
How I am that, which I propose.

Vocations

Assassins, certain to be caught
But certain of at least one shot,
Obliterate all other thought.

Torturers who come to budge
Faith like mountains, bear no grudge:
Never question, never judge.

Hunters hungry for the kill
And scenting blood and panic still
Discipline rapacious will.

Cuckolds, husbanding their pain,
Swear they will not care again,
Once the paramour is slain.

None of us, not you, not I,
Thus instructed in the lie,
Ever needs to learn to die.

Yet even as we learn to thrive
On death, the better to survive,
Truly, Love, we come alive:

To test the vast substantial thought
And Prayer of Spenser, being taught
'... the merveiles by thy mercie wrought.';

Or echo Milton's echo sent
To choir the blinding Dove's descent,
That we might see all passion spent;

Or watch a monstrous Shakespeare gauge
Upon an inward kindled stage,
Lear's irrevocable rage

And the Arcadian Marriage feast,
Where we are celebrants at least,
Transfiguring the twoback beast;

Or worship, ardent with Jack Donne,
Lest Maidenhoodwink Three in One,
To Sacramentalize the Pun;

Or with deft, gentle Herbert take
Up paradox and praise, to slake
A poet's thirst for sweet Christ's sake;

Or witness Blake with Angel Sword
And naked Babe in One accord,
Emend himself with Holy Word;

And Human, radiant, embrace,
Assume and suffer, face to Face,
Our own Annihilation, Grace.

Evening

Homage to H.V.
> 'Give him amongst thy works a place,
> Who in them loved and sought thy face!'

A perfect equipoise, to hold
Us motionless: and to enfold
The oaks, where bolts of vital gold

Out of the unthrift Sun resist
Similitude: and we persist,
To prove the Soul anachronist

Who prior to the Wind perceives
(And by such subtlety receives)
Resuscitation of these leaves:

Who, quickened into life again,
Permits our darkening to feign
Death's immediate domain.

Reflections

An ardent volume that might take
The shape of bird or beast or man,
This cloud reflected in this lake

Is more apparent in the eye
Of the beholder in its span
Than its precursor in the sky;

This drifting image here assumes
A bright delineated form
That brightness heavenward consumes;

Except a risen wind ignite
The perfect surface in a swarm
Of riffles blazed with blinding light.

Above, more towered clouds are built.
It is not vision that we lack.
Below, upon the soft-ribbed silt,

A white, discarded, severed head
Of one once-glittered trout grins back.
Do not think kindly of the dead.

The Photograph

All is perspective. If indeed he took
Us in, my Dear, you smiling by my side,
A third observer would not have denied
That, evidently, both of us must look

Out on a common prospect: from our feet,
The vacant boardwalk stretched in silver light,
The concrete sea-wall slanted to our right,
Proceed into the middle distance, meet,

And vanish at a designated point,
Grown infinitely small within the eye
Of the beholder; mirroring the sky,
A blue abundance tumbles to anoint

The shoreline ceaselessly; and to our left a trench
Of dogwood flaming under willows. Here,
This frame of frozen vision shows the near
Filigreed cast-iron public bench

Foreshortened to an archetypal throne,
And, in a patch of shadow cast, the far
Consort's throne in silhouette. Both are,
Untenanted, untenanted. We are alone.

Vernal Pond

From maculate tapioca emerge
        tadpoles; a lakh
        of India-black
Commas that thresh round the verge

Of what, in its proper season
        flooding the sward
        becomes Lake Ward:
Deasil, for no apparent reason.

They muster by rote: their disguise is,
        like the dotard's ear
        cited by Lear,
To be all of them different sizes.

Like sperm, through fecund bodywarm
        waters they seem
        purposive stream
In ciliate flagellant swarm.

Love, they are fruit of the pulsed nightlong
        rise and fall,
        clamour we call
In another classic misnomer, song.

Aerialists

Nothing, of course, from the first, but weighed against
Such parlous folly: family; friends; and the appeal,
Not lightly to be discounted, of common sense;
And last but not least, vertigo, dreadfully real.

High in tumultuous oaks, through the wind-threshed
      tops,
Squirrels play frenzied touch-tag at dizzying speed,
Flinging contortions, black synapse across bright gaps,
One after the other; driven, if not by our need.

With a heavy deadening shudder a helicopter
Batters above us: by instinct made much afraid
One freezes against the trunk from the vast raptor,
Like a hide nailed to bark, flattened and splayed.

Another is lounged on a bough to reveal of a rear
Foot the long, delicate sole: and I did not think
Strangely to be disturbed, to discover it, bare,
Unexpectedly intimate; a naked, vaginal pink.

O lately we leaned free from the buoyant crown
Of the poised radiant Tree and forbidden flew
One void to another and Everything did Abound
Held in our perfect error perfectly true.

Present

We watch, along the sand before our feet,
A wash of flame, a dazzling sleek shine
Of toppled waves encroaching to combine
And marble and reluctantly retreat.

Far out, we see a flash of white hull heel,
Some distant brightwork blaze, a dark wave break
Into a line of fire: and so illumined, make
Amends for this true passion to reveal

And understand our verities as such:
How waters alter in diurnal sway;
Light's fluent, discontinuous display;
The kindled inundation of your touch.

Gale

You huddle against my shoulder
In the lee of a mauve quartz-
Birthmarked granite boulder,
A grain of sand of sorts.

One of Zeno's arrows,
An indivisible tanker
Crosses the wild narrows.
Eternity may canker

Love like the vast rust-
Roses along the hull.
Time of course must.
Lightly, a glutted gull,

Into the wind that stings
Tears to our eyes,
Lifting dihedral wings,
Rises, flies.

Island of Burning Water

What is that blade,
Whose bright tip is marine?

No blade: but a sail,
Which (Be not afraid!)
Has caused the blue-green
Horizon to fail.

What is unmade?

The taut seams of the seen
World. Which will prevail.

This being true,
What worlds do we prove?

The great and the small.

Am I severed from you?

That this sail shall move
O beyond recall.

What has this to do
With Death?

           Ah my Love,
Nothing at all.

Spring at the Cottage

As once, at pressures that would serve to force
Us into jelly, Beebe came to peer,
Incredulous, through bolted rounds of quartz,
Out of his cramped, deep-dangled bathysphere

At nightmare lights within the black abyss,
Fantastic-fired creatures with a need
Unfathomed heretofore to luminesce,
Coldly encounter, copulate or feed,

We stand together silently and watch,
Long after the last chill light has gone,
Beyond the rippled glass, a tracking batch
Of fireflies' pulsed spangle on the lawn:

And have exhaustive knowledge found to prove
Specific-coded, heatless fire to be,
Like truth in season and like other love,
But intermittent intermittently.

Resort

A swarm of red ants, organized by God
Knows what complexities, is harvesting the small,
Sere ocotillo leaves from where they fall
Upon the desert aggregate. An odd

Meanderer, a straggler from the file,
Investigates my naked big toe, finds
It not yet to his liking, weaves, and winds
His random way across the blue-crazed tile

That, blazing, snakes about the kidney-shaped,
Almost blood-warm, turquoise swimming pool.
I bask, as if a sybaritic fool,
Who contemplates the winter death escaped:

And tell, replenishing, as they proceed
In bright succession from the muzzled drain
To form, elongate, fall, and form again,
Each perfect prism-fired water-bead.

Gravity

Now, as a level brook, that makes its way
By seeming indirection through a stand
Of tangled willows must at length betray
The certain inclination of the land,

And by erosion at some bends reveal,
Enmeshed, those roots whose deep tenacity
And thirst sustains their reaching trees, I feel
Desire's momentum, gathering what might be

The burden of the gesture that you made,
Provocative and secret as the light
That for a single burnished instant played
About your groin as we prepare for night:

Wherein, like bright roots married, we may merge;
Or streams that on immensity converge.

Faustus Wounded

No simples concocted; no more of the silent
  mendacities. For by night we behold
  the most luminous Body displayed,

The proliferation of different Fire
  in the mutual eye, in Intellectual Love!
  O small wonder we quicken to capture

The given prefigured myriad Creature,
  our Other than Other, our Dear present
  lethal cause for rejoicing, rejoicing

That over us now arches our actual Saviour.

Conjuror with Doves

Quicken! O subtle, summoned!
Here I am immobile, here I shall remember
Our multiple terror:

Beat, beads of bright blood, upwards above
The quivering, sprawled circles
Of overlapped brightness

Your bright perturbation,
My living beseeched secrets;
Let nothing at last be revealed

While they are present, delighted,
Bewildered, rapt and beholden O
Burnish darkness inwards an instant,

Vanish. After, a single
White evident feather drifts, settles
Through silence, cherished.

Faustus Analogous

Prayer is reciprocal, unheard.
I reconnoitre the absurd
Annihilation of the word.

How shall I suffer, who began
With this ignition, yoked to man,
Become unsteady in the span?

Is this imperative, Love, mine?
The consummation and divine
Profanation of the wine,

The broken healing of the bread,
Is but embodiment, the said
Devotions of the severed dead

If all is altered; to my shame
I am identical, the same
In having nothing to my name,

Save for the imprecisioned one
Now and forever just begun
Circumscription of the sun.

River

The Sun is hovered just above
Not Lethe, but the nine-ringed Styx:
Where irresistible below
The weir divided currents flow,
The muscled-under river slicks
Its brilliant surface, Love.

Is Creaturehood infatuate?
And shall we stand transfixed before
The bright dilation of a swan
Who preens her ivory upon
The nubbled emerald of the shore?
We have ourselves to hate.

Reflection harries us too soon,
Lest we succumb, to bear in mind
Upon the waters' glass the swirled
And damaged circles of this world;
Or in Her flakes of Fire find
The phases of the Moon.

Cold Lovers

Under the heaven-sent
but consumed moon,
we lie together, spent
too soon, too soon

To kindle where we one
another keep,
having banked the sun
just before sleep.

Cleave, Love: although
this mute truce we know
of Heaven must be so,

Time alone will tell
the syllables of Hell
where like and like repel.

You wake me dreaming
another, aggrieved
and mortal, seeming

Wed to Death: O forsaking
ourselves cleaved,
I dream You waking!

Lunatic in Slumber

Woman, with me, ceaseless, grieve:
The glaring error I retrieve
Is you reflect. With no reprieve,
I am, abandoned here to keep
The monstrous creaturedom of sleep.
And for all Innocence must weep,
Who with the molten Lion lies.

Yours is the glass where Madman scrys
The Peacock's Prism-risen Eyes
Annihilate! O Terror find
Me evident, for I am blind
In blaze of day!

        Out of my mind,
By glitter skewed, I am askance,
The simple victim of your glance:
Yet when we marry not by chance,
But by awakened, subtle choice,
You will not recognize my voice
Where, driven sane, I shall rejoice!

Pastoral

Already, despite ourselves,
Midsummer's erotic nights:
And fictions are wearing thin.

Mortal, we toss in our sleep;
Or wakened, lie perfectly still,
Breathing suspended, listening
As in terrible possible childhood:

Again, again, and again, and again,
Beyond impenetrable cedars
And over the oncebright wire
In a field of drugged scrub thorn;

Detached from the massed herd,
Darkgrazing, of slow boulders
Trailing the delicate beautiful weft,
The long moonluminous threads of spittle;

Rooted, her skull upthrust;
Spasmodic, sucking and pumping
A flayed animal bellow
Out over the desert water,
The nightlake bearing a hammered
Nacreous snake of moontrack;

As by desolation possessed,
Or by longing for other pasture,
Flysavaged, deprived of her calf,
Vastwombed, her shadow gravid,
A dehorned whitefaced cow
Bawls back the world's wound
At the tonguerough saltlick moon:

The same true moon whereunder
We reach for each other.

Emerging from Moonlight

From having marked a pattern in the snow
So recent that a froth of blood was bright
Incarnadine on ermine, he could know
How death had been accomplished in the night
From which he walked; how one resilient wing
Had buffeted a fern, whose unseen seed,
If broadcast thus, did not suffice to bring
The beast invisible in his most need
And final turmoil, violent and swift
Where muffled pinions, bracketing an end
Of legibility, had struck askance to lift
Raptor and broken quarry, to ascend
Beyond all evidence for our surmise
Into the frozen vacant morning skies.

Inuit

Nothing was spoken: but they have left her, sitting erect,
    with food and a little seal oil for the stone lamp.

She is very old, she is almost blind, she croons gently,
    song and the names of children, remembering him everything.

The dun herds pass. Ice-shagged bears smash through blizzard.
    Or travel in long, tireless, sideways slither over the glare-ice.

At the jagged horizon a great pale sun wanes, many-haloed.
    Half-shadowed, she rocks back at the lithe flame, diminishing,

And carves as she waits, from a fragment of bleached morse,
    a thin, pitted moon, a single eye for her last man.

Malmaison

Meniscus, disfigured, against all odds, again
    she is risen over the night garden, bleeding

To death: where the roses, these caught clots of light,
    are real and eluctable, too rich for mystery;

True mysteries being, held in the mind, astringent
    as Divinist's veinblood, as Wizard's tears:

Mortals who know of fatal juxtapositions; starsrime;
    lakewound arriving; the thin glitter of mica

In granite; O all the contagious moonspawn spilled
    into the open folds of this uplifted fecund rose:

And as well, of the rift, profound, that exists
    in this world, certain to be God's fault.

Phases of the Full Moon

Into configurations
of pale stars an abrupt
disc of bone.

Cold stone worn
next your flesh next
my flesh burns.

We shall be returned
in terror that light
tunnel night:

O reach out to me touch
me beheld death O
constant wanderer!

Brightness

has fallen   on water

and shattered   to fragments

discovered   coherent

in vision.

Autumn

That silvered sliver, piercing the orchard,
Low in the early evening,
Is the new moon not of its own accord.

Sad man, saddened, dazzled
By darkness, consider:
The Prophetic knows no foreboding.

And no nostalgia, especially for Innocence.
The heavenly drift is milt.
The heart is feral.

Heft in the mind, turn in the grained palm,
The flushed windfall in starlight; the ripe given;
The old plenitude of now.

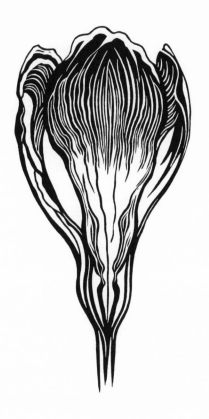

Whale on China Beach

Man added a mantissa to your bulk,
Preposterous; a bit of steel and lead
Subtracted you from life: we find you dead,
A stranded, blotched and putrefying hulk.

Conceived and carried, born, you did depend
Like us, with blooded lungs, upon the air:
Yet dwelt within a womb of waters where
You sounded depths we cannot comprehend.

Because you rolled in ardour through the seas
Wherein you were your element, and rent
The fragile purse he streams, incensed man sent
You cunning death: as if death could appease

His tangled motives or his argued right
So to despoil all creatures of their kind,
Whose being weighs no virtue in his mind,
Nor beauty correspondence in his sight.

The very oceans, endless in their sway,
Shall not contain us both. Here, where the sand
Clots shut what was your eye, we understand
This last imbalance. And silenced, turn away.

Spider in Doorway

It seems as if the morning light begets
You here, who somehow overnight have come
To rest within the latest of your sum
Of instinct-woven, geometric nets.

Insatiable for fact, we feed you true
Wonder-drugs, of which we have full range,
As an experiment, to contemplate the strange
Distortions of your orb that will ensue.

What is this reprehension, that condemns
Us, watching, while you hurriedly suck dry
Of vital nutrient a living fly,
Still struggling in the protein shroud that stems

From you without beginning, without end?
This is a death essential in its way,
Completely natural, and meaningless per se:
And it is given us, perhaps, to comprehend

How you, whose task is to perpetuate
Your kind, should so unwittingly revive
Our readiness for death, which we survive
With our ingenious webs of love and hate.

Bear

It was maintained you came, inchoate swarm,
Precocious from the womb you would escape,
And that your parent licked you into shape
Until you had assumed an ursine form.

More knowledgeable now, we understand
How you develop within narrowed chance
As zygote, foetus, cub; your winter's trance
Of hibernation; how hormones command

When you come into oestrus; how you breed;
Both where and what you forage; all your span
Of predetermined patterns. Being man,
We prize your pelt, of which we have small need.

And being man, may grieve when you are gone.
For we have learned to balance, and to frisk
In supplication, scavenge, and to risk
Our inhumanity: and dream safe dens upon

Some mountain's inaccessible, scoured shelves,
In our brief, trammelled sleep: and wake before
Each morning suffered to conceive once more
The ceaseless information of our selves.

Man in Love

Our gift is vision darkened, who first find
Ourselves discriminate, to bear in mind
Our very definition undefined.

And find the situation we have made
Unwarranted; to find ourselves dismayed
To find our subtle frailties so displayed.

Substantial, in the mind we evanesce,
And know that absolutely at a guess
We are in error constant more or less.

Then are we human in divine device,
To know our judgement, where it is most nice,
Of human kind, precisely imprecise?

The moon is silvered and the sun is seared
Within the mirror where they first appeared.
Amazed again, it is as we first feared:

Our perfect burden is not Heaven-sent.
Where we have utterance of what is meant
To be the author of the evident,

We cherish here the certainty that we
Are cherished here: and have no need to be
Enamoured of our inhumanity.

The sun has fallen, faltered that we might,
Within the darkness staggered in our sight,
Return ourselves reflected light to light.

Tree House

Eye-level with the nest
Of each harmonious bird,
Here paradigm may rest,
Secure from the absurd.

Below, on the swirled ground,
Death's variants displayed;
Above us and all around
About us is arrayed

The great tree's vital crown,
Wherein we might escape
The stark sun striking down.
One must be in good shape,

To climb the knotted rope,
Nor overcome with fear.
Do not abandon hope,
Who cannot enter here;

Leaves shall be torn away,
Fledglings must take to flight
Into the break of day,
Unto the brink of night.

Outline

I have been misinformed. For where she turned,
Foreshadowing what had not yet begun
Nor ended out of chaos, I discerned
Her least reflection dazzling the sun.

With her specific creatures in their play
Abounding, in her vivid image swirled,
I find myself configuring Glad Day
And drinking at the wellsprings of this world.

Dumbfounded here by such intelligence
And bright confusion, stricken, given pause,
Her present absence making perfect sense,
I have beheld light vacant where she was.

And where she is in clarity, God knows:
Which time, of Christ's correction, will disclose.

Sophia

When the Rose sun set
fire to earth she
ceased dreaming Him
past pain:
&
When the scabbed man rose
broken on water
reflected reflected
began again:
&
When the true moon waned
and Glad Day pierced
darkness gold spoke
on spoke
&
At last the first Sun
rose firing entire
the firmament awoke,
awoke!

Salamander

First Word
I am overheard.

I am here & there
Nowhere nowhere.

Save now & then
I am where & when.

I am why proved.
I am Love Loved.

Contents

Answers to *Riddles for Old Cameron*

1   Feather

2   Mirror

3   Rope

4   A Riddle of Claret

Wood Engravings

Barbara Howard, R.C.A., A.O.C.A., painter, engraver and graphic artist, lives and works in Toronto.